FIRST NATIONS OF NORTH AMERICA

SUBARCTIC PEOPLES

ROBIN S. DOAK

HEINEMANN LIBRARY
CHICAGO, ILLINOIS

H www.heinemannraintree.com
Visit our website to find out
more information about
Heinemann-Raintree books.

To order:
☎ Phone 888-454-2279
🖳 Visit www.heinemannraintree.com
to browse our catalog and order online.

Original illustrations © Capstone Global Library, Ltd.
Illustrated by Mapping Specialists, Ltd.
Originated by Capstone Global Library, Ltd.
Printed by China Translation and Printing Company

15 14 13 12
10 9 8 7 6 5 4 3 2

Library of Congress Cataloging-in-Publication Data
Doak, Robin S. (Robin Santos), 1963-

Subarctic peoples / Robin S. Doak.

p. cm.—(First nations of North America)

Includes bibliographical references and index.

ISBN 978-1-4329-4954-9 (hc)—ISBN 978-1-4329-4965-5
(pb) 1. Indians of North America—Canada, Northern—Juvenile literature. 2. Indians of North America—Alaska—Juvenile
literature. I. Title.

E78.C2D53 2012

971.9'01—dc22   2010042643

Acknowledgments

The author and publisher are grateful to the following for
permission to reproduce copyright material:

Alamy: p. 24 (© INTERFOTO); AP Photo: p. 40 (Jeffrey
Ulbrich); Corbis: 14 (© National Geographic Society), 29
(© Christopher J. Morris), 35 (© Corbis), 39 (© Laurent
Gillieron/epa); Getty Images: pp. 5 (Danita Delimont), 10
(Stephen J. Krasemann), 19 (Bert Garai), 31 (Emily Riddell);
istockphoto: p. 36 (© Dan Driedger); Library of Congress
Prints and Photographs Division: p. 4; Nativestock.com: pp.
15 (© Marilyn Angel Wynn), 16 (© Marilyn Angel Wynn),
26 (© Marilyn Angel Wynn), 27 (© Marilyn Angel Wynn),
28 (© Marilyn Angel Wynn), 33 (© Marilyn Angel Wynn);
Photolibrary: pp. 11 (Nativestock Pictures/Marilyn Angel
Wynn), 13 (The Print Collector), 17 (Nativestock), 22
(Thorsten Milse), 23 (Marilyn Angel Wynn), 30 (Nativestock
Pictures), 38 (Thorsten Milse), 41 (Brian Summers);
Shutterstock: p. 21 (© Morgan Lane Photography); SuperStock:
pp. 18 (IndexStock / SuperStock), 34 (© Christie's Images,
Ltd.); The Granger Collection, NYC: pp. 12, 20, 32.

Cover photograph of a Cree quilled hide pouch reproduced
with permission from SuperStock (© Christie's Images, Ltd.).

We would like to thank Peter Collings,Ph.D., for his invaluable
help in the preparation of this book.

Contents

Some words are shown in bold **like this**. You can find out what they mean by looking in the glossary.

Who Were the First People in North America?

In 1980 native peoples throughout Canada adopted a **resolution**. It said, in part:

> We, the original people of this land know the Creator put us here.... The Creator gave us our spiritual beliefs, our languages, our **culture**, and a place on Mother Earth which provided us with all our needs.... The rights and responsibilities given to us by the Creator cannot be altered or taken away by any other **Nation**.

More than 12,000 years ago, people lived throughout North America. The earliest peoples made their homes in every part of the continent, from icy northern regions to hot, humid regions in the southern part of the continent. But, after European explorers began arriving there in the late 1400s, other groups began laying claim to North America.

◄ Some of the earliest peoples in North America settled in the Subarctic region of the continent.

◄ The descendants of the first peoples to live in the Subarctic region of Alaska and Canada continue to follow long-standing traditions.

Native Americans or American Indians?

In 1492 Italian explorer Christopher Columbus arrived in the Americas. Believing he had found Asia, which was then called the Indies, he used the name "Indian" for the peoples who were living in the region. For centuries, all of the first peoples of the Americas were known as Indians.

The term "American Indian" was used for many years. "Native American" was introduced in the late 1900s honoring the fact that these were the first humans to live in the region. Most native peoples, however, would rather be identified by their **tribe** or nation—for example, Ojibwa.

Today, **descendants** of the earliest Subarctic peoples live and work in the same areas where their **ancestors** first settled. In Alaska, these people are known as Alaskan Native. In Canada, they are the First Nations people.

5

Who were the first people in North America?

The first people to settle in North America **migrated** from Asia. Scientists believe they arrived on foot, following the herds of mammoths, reindeer, and other large animals they hunted for food and clothing. They traveled from one continent to the other over the **Bering Land Bridge**, a 1,000-mile (1,600-kilometer) stretch of land that connected Asia to North America. This pathway existed during the last Ice Age, between 10,000 and 25,000 years ago.

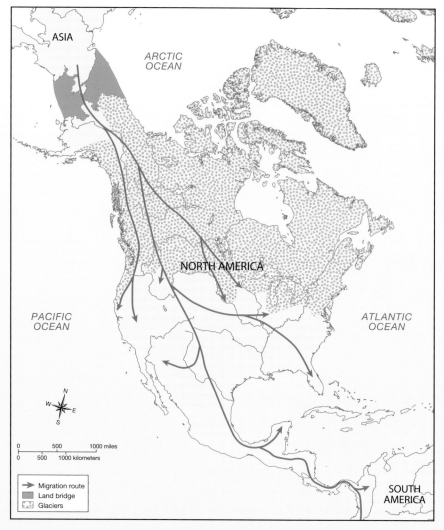

◄ This map shows some of the routes early peoples took as they spread across North America.

◀ People who lived near each other often shared the same language and customs. The areas where these people lived—including the Subarctic—are known as **culture areas**.

The new arrivals, known today as **Paleo-Indians**, spread throughout North America. Some headed into present-day Mexico and beyond. Other groups made their homes on the **plains**. Still others settled on the east and west coasts of the continent, becoming farmers and cultivating crops of squash, corn, and beans.

The Subarctic

Scientists believe that the Subarctic region was one of the first areas to be settled in North America. The Subarctic is a 3,000-mile (4,800-kilometer) band of **boreal forests** stretching across the northern part of the continent. It includes most of present-day Canada and parts of Alaska. Fewer early peoples lived in the Subarctic than in other regions in North America.

The Ice Age came to an end and temperatures rose. Ice glaciers melted and ocean levels rose. The Bering Land Bridge eventually disappeared. People, animals, and plants stopped migrating from Asia to North America.

Who Are the Peoples of the Subarctic?

In the Subarctic, the first settlers lived together in small groups called **bands**. Each band was made up of one or more families. A band might have as many as 30 people. Bands that lived in the same area were known as a **tribe**. Bands within the tribe shared the same language and customs. They also shared hunting territories and sometimes lived together in seasonal camps.

In recent years, some tribes have banded together and formed **nations**. They did this in order to protect their land and customs. For example, the Dene Nation is made up of tribes in the **Northwest Territories**, an area in northern Canada.

Major groups

There are two major groups of Subarctic peoples within the region. Those who live in the eastern part of the region (see the map at right) speak Algonquian languages. They include the Cree, Innu, Ojibwa, and Algonquin peoples. In the western part of the region, many Subarctic peoples spoke Athabaskan languages. These groups include the peoples of the Dene Nation as well as Alaskan Athabaskan people.

Another distinct group within the Subarctic region is the **Métis**. They are the **descendants** of both First Nations people and Europeans. The Métis speak a language that includes native, French, and English words.

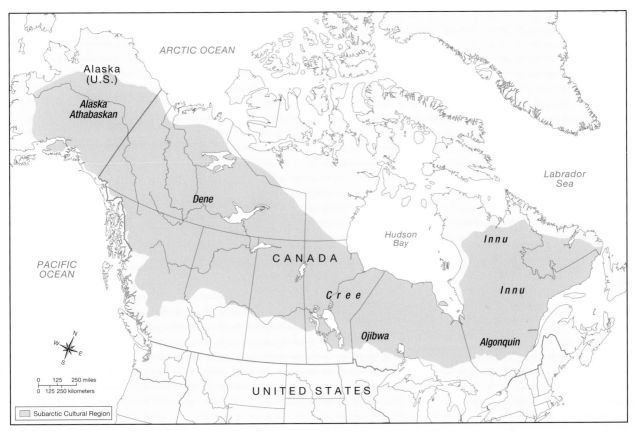

▲ Subarctic bands lived throughout central Alaska and much of Canada.

LANGUAGE

What's in a Name?

The word "Dene" is an Athabaskan term that means "the people." The Dene call their homeland Denendeh, which means "the Creator's Spirit flows through this Land."

The boreal forest

The Subarctic region is made up of the **boreal forest** of North America. The boreal forest, sometimes called the taiga, stretches across the interior of Alaska and Canada. It is wedged between two areas. To the north is the Arctic **tundra**. Tundra is flat, frozen, treeless land. To the south are **plains**, forests, and mountains.

The boreal forest is made up of evergreen trees, including spruce, birch, pine, and fir. Winters in the forest are long, cold, and snowy. Temperatures average around 14°F (-10°C). In many places the ground is covered with a layer of permanently frozen soil called **permafrost**. Summers are short, with temperatures hovering around 72°F (22°C).

▲ The Subarctic region is made up of lakes, rivers, and forests filled with evergreen trees such as pines and firs.

▲ Subarctic bands adapted to their local surroundings.

Surviving in the boreal forest

Because of the long winters, farming was not possible for early Subarctic peoples. Instead, they relied on hunting and gathering to survive. The forests were home to many different kinds of animals. Large **game** included moose and caribou. Early peoples trapped smaller animals, such as beavers, rabbits, fox, and otters, for food and clothing. They also hunted birds.

The many rivers and lakes throughout the region were a source of fish, including trout, salmon, and pike. During the summer, bands would camp together by the water and fish and hunt together. People also gathered berries and roots to eat.

What Was an Early Subarctic Village Like?

Early Subarctic peoples did not live in permanent villages. Instead, they traveled between winter and summer camps. They moved from one place to the other to take advantage of the most plentiful food sources. In the winter, many **bands** hunted the **migrating** caribou. In the summer, they traveled to rivers and lakes to fish.

Because they were constantly on the move, early Subarctic peoples had few possessions. Most of their goods were things that were necessary, such as clothing, hunting tools, and the items they needed to build their next shelters. When they left one camp for the next, they had to pack up and carry all of their belongings.

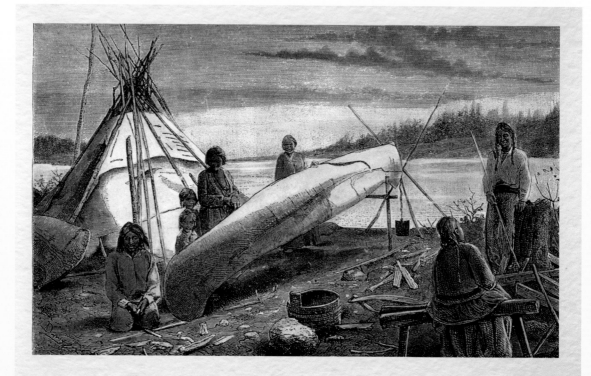

▲ Subarctic families lived together in groups called bands.

▲ Family life was very important to early Cree Indians, as it is to modern Crees today.

Families in the Subarctic

The family was the most important unit for Subarctic bands. Families included grandparents, a husband and wife, and children. In some bands, two families that were related to one another lived together in one dwelling. If members of a band were too closely related, they were not allowed to marry one another.

The villages did not have a **chief**. Instead, the members of a band or **tribe** looked to the person who was the wisest and who could lead the others in times of trouble. This leader might make decisions about warfare and trading. However, his power came from the entire band. If members of the band did not agree with the leader, they did not have to follow his advice.

Subarctic tipis and lean-tos

People in the Subarctic used the resources available in the **boreal forest** to construct their houses. Most homes were constructed of wood, animal **hides**, and dirt. All of the homes were fast and simple to build and take down.

One of the most common types of Subarctic homes was the **tipi**. Tipis were tentlike dwellings that were made with a frame of wooden poles or branches. The frame was then covered with either animal hides or tree bark. Some tipis were cone-shaped, while others were dome-shaped. All tipis were portable and easy to put up, take down, and transport.

Another type of summer home was the **lean-to**. This open-faced, temporary shelter was made with branches and leaves. Larger families might build a double lean-to, with two lean-tos facing each other. A single fire, lit in the center, was used for warmth, light, and cooking.

▲ Among the Cree, women made and owned the tipis.

▲ This Cree home is covered with caribou skins.

Log houses, pit houses, and sweathouses

In the winter, some bands moved into sturdy, cone-shaped log houses. These homes had roofs of dirt and snow. Subarctic peoples wedged moss in the gaps of the logs to keep the cold and wind from entering. Other groups built **pit houses** in the winter. These were dug partially into the ground and covered with a roof of dirt, snow, and branches.

A **sweathouse** was a special dome-shaped structure covered with robes and blankets. A hole dug in the middle of the house was filled with hot stones and covered with wet moss. The steam was believed to cure illnesses and purify the body.

What Did Early Subarctic Peoples Eat?

The early peoples of the Subarctic were hunters and gatherers. Among their chief sources of food were the caribou and moose that lived in the region. Some groups, like the Chipewyan, depended upon caribou completely. They were **nomadic**, following the animals as they **migrated** from place to place.

Because the caribou were difficult to successfully hunt, **bands** of Subarctic peoples often came together to share hunting grounds. They would camp at the same sites and work together to make sure that their people did not go hungry. Bands hunted, fished, and lived side by side.

▲ Several bands of Subarctic hunters would often work together to corral and kill caribou.

▲ In addition to trapping and fishing, women also cut up, prepared, and stored food for their band.

Who hunted for food?

Men were in charge of hunting and killing the big animals. Sometimes they built pens called **corrals** out of tree branches. Some groups scared the caribou into the corrals, where the hunters used spears, bows and arrows, and knives to kill them. After Subarctic peoples began trading with French and English fur traders (see pages 32 to 35), they used guns to kill the animals.

Women played an important role in finding and preparing food. They hunted smaller animals, including rabbits, birds, and fish. They created traps to catch small **game**, and they wove nets and baskets to trap and store fish. Cree women followed the men as they hunted buffalo. When a buffalo was killed, the women would go to work. They cut up the animal and carried it back to camp.

▲ The hides of animals were scraped free of fur, then used to make clothing and baskets.

Respecting nature

The Subarctic peoples believed that to be successful hunters, they must respect the animals they hunted. All animals were believed to have a soul or spirit. Many bands performed **rituals** before and after the hunt to calm the animal spirits. During the rituals, they thanked the animal for allowing itself to be caught and killed.

Early peoples put nearly every part of the dead animal to use. They used the meat and organs for food. They turned furs and **hides** into clothing, blankets, and tent coverings. They used bones and antlers to make tools, or they carved them into pieces of art. They even used the animals' stomach lining as storage containers for berries and other items.

Gathering and storing food

Although they did not farm, the peoples of the Subarctic collected the many berries and edible plants that grew throughout the region. They ate blueberries, cranberries, raspberries, and strawberries, along with roots, barks, and herbs. Sometimes they mixed the berries with fat and dried fish or meat. This food, which lasted for months, was called **pemmican**. Berries and roots were also used to make medicines to cure diarrhea and other ailments.

Subarctic peoples stored food to help them survive the long winters. They placed dried fish, caribou, and other meats in storage places called **caches**. Some caches were pits dug into the ground. Others were platforms built high in the branches of a tree.

◄ Subarctic peoples caught fish using woven baskets and nets, as well a hooks and lines.

How Did Early Subarctic Peoples Travel?

Travel was the key to survival for most Subarctic **bands**. The most common form of travel was by foot. When the time came to move to a new camp, all of the band's goods—clothing, tents, and hunting tools—were packed up and loaded to be transported. In Chipewyan groups, the women were responsible for toting all the goods. This left the men free to hunt as they traveled.

Because of large amounts of standing water, summertime travel could be difficult. Subarctic peoples used the rivers and lakes as pathways. They built sturdy **canoes** out of birch bark. Birch bark is hard, lightweight, and waterproof. The bark was attached to cedar pieces that had been soaked in water and shaped to form the canoe's skeleton. Canoes were also used for fishing and hunting caribou.

▲ To carry heavy loads, some Subarctic peoples used a **tumpline**. This is a headband that is used to support a load and make it easier to carry.

▲ Each region of the Subarctic had its own style of snowshoe. Most were narrow, with the toe turned up.

Winter travel

Early Subarctic peoples created special equipment to help them get around in the winter. The Subarctic peoples invented sleds called **toboggans** to carry goods through the snow. Other groups made snowshoes out of birch and animal **hides**. The hides were used to create the snowshoe netting. Early Subarctic peoples wore the snowshoes while hunting and gathering food. They also created snow goggles to cut down on the glare of sunlight on snow.

What Clothing Did Early Subarctic Peoples Wear?

Like other native peoples, early Subarctic **bands** used the animals they hunted to make clothing. Moose and caribou **hides** were among the most common sources of shirts, dresses, **tunics**, leggings, and **moccasins**. Women prepared the hides for sewing by scraping them first to remove the hair. Then some bands soaked the skins in animal brains to make them soft.

While summer clothing was lightweight, winter fashions were warmer and heavier. Women made fur coats, robes, and sleeping garments out of beaver and rabbit fur. Moccasins were replaced with fur-lined boots.

▶ Winter clothing was designed to protect people from the cold and snow.

Decorating clothes and bodies

The clothes of early Subarctic peoples were functional. But many things they wore were also beautiful. Women decorated their clothing with porcupine quills, animal teeth, and beads made out of seeds they collected. They dyed their clothes with berries and clay. Some bands wore hats and jewelry. Subarctic jewelry was made out of shells, antlers, and even bear claws.

Subarctic peoples took great pride in their appearance. Men plucked the hair from their faces. Men and women alike rubbed animal fat into their hair and skin to make it soft and shiny. Some **tribes** tattooed or painted their faces and other parts of the body. Body paint was made of clay mixed with fat.

Baby fashion

In some areas, Subarctic babies wore diapers made of animal hides. The diapers were stuffed with moss to absorb wetness. Infants throughout the Subarctic spent the first months of their lives strapped into a **cradleboard**. This was a board with a sack for the baby that was worn on the mother's back.

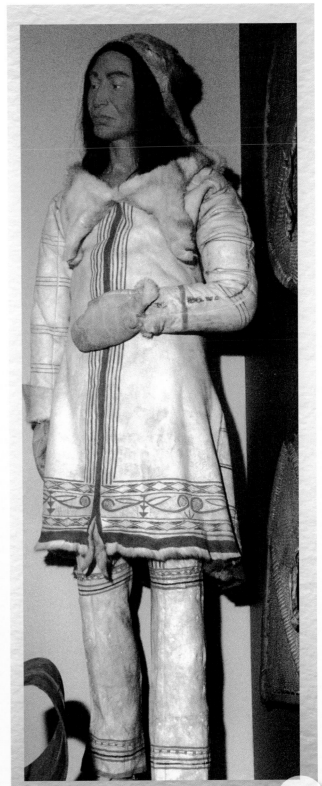

▶ Subarctic groups often decorated their clothing. These clothes are made from caribou hide and then painted with designs.

23

What Did Early Subarctic Peoples Believe?

Early Subarctic peoples believed that all living things in the world around them had spirits. They believed that these spirits could help or harm them—depending upon whether the spirit was good or bad. They prayed to the spirits for health, successful hunting, and protection from evil.

A spiritual leader helped connect people to the unseen world. The leader was believed to have been given special powers by the spirits.

▲ This Chippewa healer sucks disease out of a patient with a bone.

"How Wisagatcak Flooded the World": A Cree Folktale

The following is a Cree story that explains the creation of the world. Wisagatcak, the Cree trickster, wanted to capture the Great Beaver. The trickster threw his spear at the animal, but missed. Beaver wanted revenge. He created a huge dam, which caused a flood that destroyed the world.

As the water levels rose, Wisagatcak built a raft and put all the animals of Earth on it. After spending several days floating, the trickster placed moss on the surface of the raft. The moss grew and grew until it created a whole new world.

The spiritual leader used his or her powers to communicate with the spirits and also to heal the sick. During healing **ceremonies**, he or she sang and danced. He or she might massage or blow on the suffering person. The spiritual leader also knew which berries, roots, and barks to use for medicines.

Spirits, heroes, and tricksters

Some groups believed in a supreme spirit that created Earth and all things in it. Algonquian-speaking groups called this spirit the Great Manitou. Other **bands** also believed in both a hero and trickster character. The hero was the first powerful person in the world. The trickster was a mischievous spirit that could cause trouble for humans. Both the hero and the trickster helped form the world.

What Did Early Subarctic Peoples Do to Celebrate?

Subarctic **bands** often came together seasonally to share good hunting and fishing grounds. But these meetings were about more than just work. Subarctic peoples used the gatherings as a chance to hold festivals, **ceremonies**, and **rituals** and to celebrate being together.

One important celebration for the Alaskan Athabaskan people was the **potlatch**. This was a ceremony of feasting and gift giving. It could be held to honor the dead. A potlatch also marked a special occasion, such as when a boy took part in his first hunt. Other potlatches were held by one band to show visiting bands how prosperous they were. Alaskan Athabaskan people continue this celebration today.

▲ Seasonal hunting camps brought people from different bands together for work and for play.

In the past, potlatch ceremonies could last for up to a week. During that time, native peoples sang, danced to the beat of drums, and ate. The Alaskan Athabaskan people even built a special building for the potlatch. Potlatches are still held by Alaskan Athabaskan people today.

The Sun Dance

Another important ceremony was the Sun Dance, also called the Thirst Dance. During this ritual, men of the **tribe** did not eat or drink anything for several days. They stayed out in the hot Sun until they had a vision. In Cree bands, the men pierced their own skin with a horn and attached themselves to a pole. They danced, tugged, and twisted until the horn ripped free from their skin. Sun Dances are still held in Canada today.

▶ This Chippewa man dances in a traditional celebration. Subarctic peoples today carry on the traditions of their **ancestors**.

27

A DAY IN THE LIFE OF A CREE YOUNG PERSON

Today is a special day for the teen. Like his father and grandfather before him, the boy will begin his **vision quest**. The vision quest is a **ritual** that all boys must undergo. When it is over, he will no longer be considered a boy. Instead, his **band** members will look at him as a man.

The boy has been preparing for this moment all his life. As a child, he watched and listened as the band's **elders** taught him how to survive in the forest. His uncle taught him how to find his way home when he was lost. His father told him about the caribou and moose. He explained the animals' habits and where to find them.

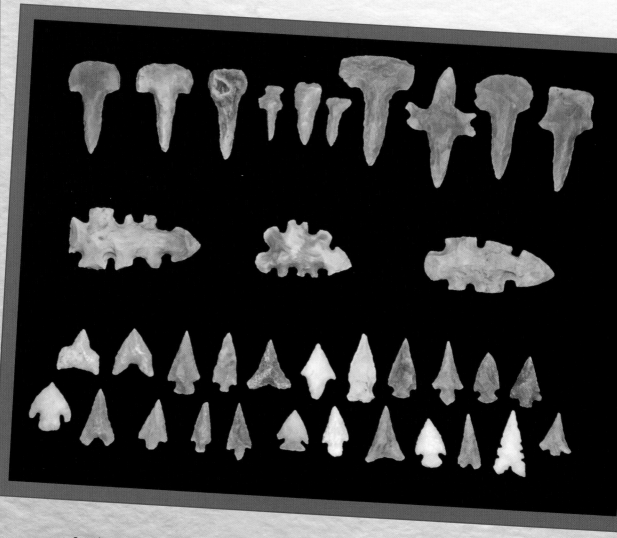

▲ Cree boys were taught to create arrowheads and other weapons for hunting.

▲ Subarctic children of today are learning to preserve their heritage.

The boy and his friends also practiced the skills they would need as adults. While his sister learned to sew and to cut up rabbits and other small **game**, he shot bows and arrows at a target. Games like stickball, played with a caribou-**hide** ball stuffed with moss, helped the boy become well coordinated.

Now, the boy and his father have arrived at the abandoned bear den. The two smoke a pipe together. The boy is left alone. He will stay here, **fasting** and praying, for days. If he is successful, the young man will eventually have a vision. He will find his spirit helper. He believes this spirit will help him get through life without harm. Only then will he return home and take his place—as an adult—among his band.

What Art and Music Did Early Subarctic Peoples Create?

The items early Subarctic peoples chose to move from camp to camp were often both useful and beautiful. They decorated clothing, tents, and other everyday items, making them works of art.

▲ This Chippewa woman weaves a mat for the inside of her home.

A Subarctic Art Form

Subarctic artists are best known for their elaborate embroidery and beading. In earlier times, the Dene, Alaskan Athabaskan, and other groups sewed geometric patterns and pictures of flowers and animals onto their clothing.

They also decorated shirts, robes, and coats with fringes, porcupine quills, animal teeth, and the seeds of local plants. After contact with Europeans, they began making artwork with the glass beads they got from trading.

▲ Cree and other Subarctic peoples continue to create beautiful beaded items today.

Early craftspeople made baskets with animal **hides**, reeds, and other items. These baskets were used for storage and to carry goods. But many were also decorated with woven patterns and colorful dyes. Subarctic peoples throughout the region continue to craft baskets today.

Painting is another traditional form of Subarctic art. Early peoples in the region painted on hides, birch bark, clothing, and even their **tipis**. They used paints and dyes made of berries and clay.

Music

Music is important to the Subarctic peoples, too. Drums made of animal hide and wood were the most common early musical instrument. They were used during religious **ceremonies** as well as festive occasions such as the **potlatch**. Later, Subarctic peoples were introduced to fiddles by French and Scots traders. They soon incorporated fiddling into their ceremonies and began creating their own folk songs, which are still sung today.

How Did Subarctic Peoples Interact with Nonnatives?

Europeans first entered the Subarctic region in the early 1500s. These first visitors were French and English explorers and fur traders. They came looking for the **hides** of foxes, rabbits, caribou, and especially beavers. People in Europe used the furs for hats, coats, boots, and other items.

In 1608 French explorer Samuel de Champlain founded Quebec City, the first permanent European settlement in present-day Canada. French fur traders, called **voyageurs**, set out from there and from other later settlements to trade with the peoples of the Subarctic. In 1611 English explorer Henry Hudson came into contact with the Cree people in the James Bay region of Canada. He then staked an English claim to the area.

▲ This illustration depicts Pierre-Esprit Radisson, a French explorer and trader, meeting Subarctic traders.

Trade

In the early 1670s, an English company called the Hudson's Bay Company set up trading posts throughout the region. Several Algonquian-speaking groups moved from their traditional campsites to be closer to the trading posts. They began to change their seasonal patterns of hunting and fishing, to have better opportunities to trade with the Europeans.

In the coming years, both the Cree and Ojibwa would serve as important **middlemen** between the Europeans and native **bands** throughout the region. They carried weapons, clothing, and beads to Subarctic peoples, trading them for the furs that the Europeans prized.

▲ Subarctic peoples traded animal furs such as these for goods such as beads and items made from metal.

Major changes

The arrival of European settlers and traders changed the way most Subarctic bands lived. Many **tribes** began to rely on the European trade goods they received in exchange for animal skins and furs. Bands began using guns to hunt animals instead of the traditional spears, and bows and arrows. Many Subarctic peoples stopped wearing the traditional animal-hide clothing, preferring instead to make their garments out of the cloth supplied by European traders.

◄ European goods changed some aspects of Subarctic peoples' lives such as how they dressed.

The Europeans also tried to influence relations within and between bands. Traders attempted to set up **chiefs** within each native band. They hoped that this would make it easier for them to control trade through the chief they had chosen. Some Europeans even took up arms in native conflicts. In 1609, for example, Champlain and French troops helped the Algonquin defeat their enemy, the Iroquois.

Problems

The contact with Europeans came at a cost. In the 1800s and 1900s, peoples throughout the region suffered from **discrimination**, or unfair treatment. They lost their lands to nonnative settlers. They also faced pressure from **missionaries**, politicians, and educators to give up their native religions, languages, and customs and adopt the ways of the Canadian and U.S. people.

BIOGRAPHY

Louis Riel: Métis Champion

Louis Riel (1844–1885) was the **descendant** of native and French-Canadian people. In 1869 Riel organized **Métis** people living in the Red River Settlement in present-day Manitoba, Canada.

Together, Riel and the Métis prevented the Canadian government from taking control of Métis land. In 1885 Riel was hanged after leading a second, less successful rebellion.

▶ Louis Riel helped found the **province** of Manitoba and served as one of its leaders.

What Have Subarctic Peoples Contributed to the World?

Subarctic peoples have left their mark on other **cultures** since the first Europeans arrived. The earliest French and English traders to visit the region adopted native **canoe**, snowshoe, and clothing designs in order to better adapt to life in their new homes. They relied on native peoples to guide them through the region. They needed to learn about the animals of the **boreal forests** and about the local rivers and lakes.

▲ Some of the first people to use toboggans were the First **Nations** people of Canada. Now people all over the world use **toboggans**.

Native Names

Places throughout Canada and Alaska still bear the names given to them by the native peoples of the Subarctic region. Here are just a few:

Manitoba: This comes from a Cree or Ojibwa word meaning "strait of the spirit."

Quebec: This comes from an Algonquian word meaning "where the river narrows."

Saskatchewan: This comes from a Cree word meaning "swift-flowing river."

Saskatoon: This comes from a Cree word meaning "early berries."

Winnipeg: This comes from Cree words meaning "muddy water."

Yukon: This comes from a Gwich'in word meaning "great river."

People today still use gear that was originally designed by Subarctic peoples. In the winter, for example, adults and children alike enjoy using snowshoes and toboggans for fun. In the summer, people paddle canoes that are still very similar in design to early Subarctic ones.

Language

Many words of the Subarctic peoples have been adopted into the English language and are used today. These words include "canoe," "chipmunk," "toboggan," and "totem."

Arts and crafts

Subarctic arts and crafts are popular with people near and far. The **Métis's** capes, purses, jewelry, and clothing are highly valued. Cree artists also create popular pieces of art made by chewing a pattern onto birch bark. A number of Subarctic artists have recently attracted worldwide attention.

Where Are Subarctic Peoples Today?

People who are **descendants** of early Subarctic peoples continue to make their homes in Canada and Alaska. In the **Northwest Territories**, half of all people living there are descendants of native peoples. In all, nearly 4 percent of Canada's population is made up of descendants of the region's first peoples.

Reserves

Less than half of all native peoples in Canada live on **reserves**. A reserve is an area of land that has been set aside by the Canadian government. There are more than 2,000 such areas throughout Canada, covering more than 6 million acres (2.4 million hectares) of land.

▲ Some reserves are far away and difficult to reach.

▲ These Cree representatives attend a meeting at the United Nations headquarters in Geneva, Switzerland.

On the reserves, people work to balance modern ways with the older, more traditional ways. **Canoes** have been replaced in some areas by boats with motors. Instead of sled dogs, some Subarctic peoples use snowmobiles to drag **toboggans** to help them get around in the winter.

Keeping traditions alive

The Cree people make up the largest native group in Canada. They keep their **culture** alive by teaching Cree ways to the young and the Cree language in schools. Some Cree have gained positions in government in order to make their voices heard.

Most Subarctic peoples live in towns and cities throughout Canada. It is often easier to find jobs and earn a living there. But away from other members of their **tribe**, it is also easier for them to forget the old ways. It is a challenge for these people to keep long-standing traditions alive.

Taking care of the land

One of the challenges native peoples face today is protecting their lands from development. As the demand for natural resources like wood, oil, and electricity increases, non-natives have tried to **exploit** the land where native peoples have lived for centuries. Many Subarctic peoples have joined forces to fight for protection of their lands.

▲ The James Bay Project is destroying lands that once belonged to native peoples. The Grand Council of the Crees was formed to help fight for Crees' rights to their lands.

▲ Subarctic young people are taught traditional customs, as well as modern technology.

In Canada, some **bands** are working with mining, timber, and power companies. The Innu in some regions, for example, are making agreements that ensure their land is used carefully and respectfully. They also want to benefit from any use of their land.

First Nations

Canada's native peoples have banded together to make sure their concerns are heard. More than 600 bands call themselves the First **Nations**. (The term does not include the Inuit or the **Métis**.) The term emphasizes the common background and traditions that the bands and tribes share. It also highlights their desire to be recognized as the native peoples of the region. By standing together, First Nations people have successfully stopped development that would have harmed the land they have lived on for centuries.

In the coming years, the people of the Subarctic region will continue to face challenges from people who want to use their land. They must find ways to make sure that the ancient ways are remembered and passed on to future generations.

Timeline

about 10,000 BCE   People from Asia cross the **Bering Land Bridge** to North America.

1492 CE   Christopher Columbus reaches the Americas. He calls the people he meets there Indians, a name that is still used in some areas today.

1608   French explorer Samuel de Champlain founds Quebec City, the first permanent European settlement in Canada.

1609   Champlain and French troops help the Algonquin defeat their enemy, the Iroquois.

1611   Henry Hudson, on his last voyage to North America, comes into contact with the Cree of James Bay.

early 1670s   The Hudson's Bay Company sets up trading posts throughout the Subarctic region.

1869   **Métis** leader Louis Riel organizes a successful resistance in present-day Manitoba, Canada.

1885   After leading an unsuccessful armed rebellion in the **Northwest Territories**, Riel is hanged for treason (being disloyal) by the Canadian government.

mid-1900s   Many Subarctic peoples move to cities, seeking work after the fur trade ends.

1971   The Alaska Native Claims Settlement Act gives land and money to Native Alaskans.

1985   Canada revises its Indian Act to remove sections that caused **discrimination** and to give back native rights and status.

1994   Cree and other native peoples temporarily halt a massive **hydroelectric** project in Quebec called the James Bay Project.

2001   Cree people, Quebec officials, and government officials sign an agreement to use native land to create hydroelectric power.

2007   First **Nations** people organize a demonstration called the Aboriginal Day of Action to bring attention to poverty, lack of health care, and other native issues.

Glossary

ancestor family member from the distant past

band Indian family group that lived together

Bering Land Bridge stretch of land, 1,000 miles (1,600 kilometers) long, that once connected Asia to North America

boreal forest northern forest made up of coniferous and evergreen trees

cache place to store food and other goods

canoe light, narrow boat

ceremony religious event or observance

chief leader of a group of people

corral pen used to capture animals like caribou

cradleboard device made from a board and a sack and worn on the back for carrying an infant

culture shared ways of life and beliefs of a group of people

culture area region of North America in which Indians traditionally had a similar way of life

descendant offspring of an earlier group

discrimination act of being unfair to a person or group

elder older person

exploit use unfairly

fast to go without food

game wild animals hunted for food

hide animal skin

hydroelectric electricity created by channeling moving water

lean-to open-faced, temporary shelter made with branches and leaves

Métis people in Canada who are the descendants of both native and European people

middleman person or group who acts as a go-between for two other groups

migrate move from one place to another

missionary person who tries to persuade others to adopt his or her religion

moccasin ankle-length shoe made of animal skin

nation group of tribes that have banded together

nomadic moving from place to place without a fixed home

Northwest Territories territory in northern Canada that includes Nunavut

Paleo-Indians first people to enter and live in the Americas

pemmican long-lasting food made of berries mixed with fat and dried fish or meat

permafrost layer of permanently frozen soil

pit house home dug partially into the ground and covered with a roof of dirt, snow, and branches

plain flat stretch of land

potlatch feast held by some American Indian tribes, during which the host offers gifts to his or her guests

province administrative division of a country, similar to a state in the United States

reserve area of land given back to the native peoples of Canada by the government

resolution formal expression of opinion

ritual formal acts or series of acts performed according to a set of rules, often having to do with religion

sweathouse hut heated with steam

tipi portable, tentlike dwelling made with wooden poles and animal skins

toboggan long, flat sled with a curved front end

tribe group of American Indians who share a culture

tumpline headband used to support a load and make it easier to carry

tundra frozen plain in the Arctic regions

tunic long shirt made out of animal skins

vision quest ritual that marks the beginning of adulthood for some American Indian boys

voyageur French-Canadian fur trader

Find Out More

Books

Doherty, Craig A., and Katherine M. Doherty. *Subarctic Peoples.* New York: Chelsea House, 2010.

Howse, Jennifer. *Métis.* Calgary, Canada: Weigl, 2010.

King, David C. *First People: An Illustrated History of American Indians.* New York: Dorling Kindersley, 2008.

Murdoch, David H. *North American Indian.* New York: Dorling Kindersley, 2005.

Websites

Alaska History and Cultural Studies
www.akhistorycourse.org
This website includes information on Native Alaskans.

Innu Nation
www.innu.ca
Visit the website of the Innu nation.

Virtual Museum of Canada
www.museevirtuel-virtualmuseum.ca
This website includes the early history of Subarctic peoples.

Virtual Museum of Métis History and Culture
www.metismuseum.ca
Visit this website to learn more about the Métis people.

DVDs

Native Art of Canada. Vancouver: Daval, 2008.

Ontario, Canada's Far North—Moose Factory First Nation People. Directed by Tom Geagan. Marina del Rey, Calif.: Travelscope, 2010.

Visions from the Wilderness: The Art of Paul Kane. Directed by John Bessai. Toronto: Cinefocus, 2006.

Places to visit

Alaska Native Heritage Center
Heritage Center Dr.
Anchorage, AK
www.alaskanative.net

Canadian Museum of Civilization
Gatineau, Quebec, Canada
www.civilization.ca/cmc/home/cmc-home

National Museum of the American Indian
Fourth Street and Independence Avenue, SW
Washington, D.C.
www.nmai.si.edu

Further research

What parts of the Subarctic lifestyle did you find the most interesting? How does life for native peoples in the boreal forest compare to the way native peoples live today in other regions? How did the peoples who first lived in your area contribute to life today? To learn more about the Subarctic or other culture areas, visit one of the suggested places on these pages or head to your local library for more information.

Index